RED FIELD OF DREAMS

THE CREATOR SPEAKS

POETRY

By
W. Henry Eccleston

Gettysburg College—Civil War Institute
The poem "Embattled Fields at Gettysburg" by **W. Henry Eccleston** was the featured work at the Lincoln Civil War Institute at Gettysburg College, along with an exhibition of his paintings. On April 1, 2008, the Lincoln Prize in literature was awarded at the Yale Club. See www.gettysburg.edu/civilwar/institute and www.gettysburg.edu/library/news/exhibits/creator_speaks.dot

The National Association of Black Journalists (NABJ) Congratulates the 2011 SALUTE TO EXCELLENCE WINNERS Radio – Documentary "Curtis Mayfield - Keep on Pushin" to Sir. W. Henry Eccleston Artistic Director and Producer, Terry Wilson, Shawn Rhodes and Nate Walker... the Midnight Ravers WBAI - NY 99.5 FM

WASHINGTON, DC (August 9, 2011) - The National Association of Black Journalists (NABJ) announced today the winners for its 2011 Salute to Excellence Awards. The competition honors work from print, television, radio, online, photojournalism, and public relations. Winners were announced Saturday, August 6, 2011 at an annual gala celebration during NABJ's 36th Annual Convention and Career Fair in Philadelphia, the largest gathering of minority journalists in the country.

The poem: "Thirty Years in Brooklyn" was winner of a Gold Medal Award in Poetry from Famous Poets.

W. Henry Eccleston is a painter with international fame. How lucky that I was led to him. A man of high character. "The scholar, the artist, the humanitarian. "Mortals Mansion", a poem by him. He's "A Gift to Humanity". Crescenciana C. Ticzon-Bokhari . World Poetry Library. Texas / PHILIPPINES

First Printing 2011
ISBN: 978-0-578-09180-8
Copyright © 2005 by W. Henry Eccleston

Published by: i art i gallery.

All rights reserved. No part of this publication may be reproduced, stored in a retrieval system, or transmitted in any form or by any means mechanical, electronic, photocopy, recording or any other except for brief quotations in printed review, without the prior permission of the author and publisher.

Requests for information should be addressed to:iartigallery.com

646-853-6708 (gallery)

Henr832@aol.com

Contents

INTRODUCTION	5
ACKNOWLEDGEMENTS	7
THIRTY YEARS IN BROOKLYN	8
MUSIC OF THE SPHERE	10
SIEVE TO PURIFY	13
*SECRET MOMENTS ENJOYED	15
SECRET MOMENTS ENJOYED	16
THREAT OF THE BIG ONE	17
MORTALS MANSION	18
TRENCH TOWN REMINISCENCE	20
WEST KINGSTON GHETTO TROUBLES	22
MISSING YOU	24
MISSING YOU	25
CLARITY OF VISION	26
FRESH FACE	27
ARE YOU AWARE?	28
DO YOU FEEL THE HURT	29
THE HOUSE IN WHICH WE DWELL	30
CONVICTED, IF FOUND GUILTY	34
MY TWIN FLAME	37
RED FIELD OF DREAMS	38
BIRTHRIGHT	42
BEYOND MIND OVER MATTER	43
YOU LOVING ME FOR ME	44
VIRGIN'S BIRTH	45
DIVINE MENTOR	46

MANKIND AND HIS RACE	47
AWESOME LOVERS' RETREAT	49
TYPICAL GHETTO LIVITY	51
NATTY BONGO SPEAKS	57
PURPOSE	59
NOT WITH MY EYES	60
FRYING FISH ROUND A CANARSIE	61
REMNANT OF THE ERA DAYS	63
IMAGES OF THE HEART	64
VIRTUE	65
REGGAE ROCKS	66
IMMORTAL'S WILL	67
RASTA CO SHARES A CHURCH	68
THE PLAYGROUND OF SOULS	70
YOUR SWEET ORCHID	71
GOD'S LEISURE TIME	72
EMBATTLED FIELDS AT GETTYSBURG	74
TRANSFORMED TRENCH PEN- CREATING TRENCH TOWN	75

INTRODUCTION

Red Fields of Dreams
The Creator Speaks through Poetry

> "My work stimulates the intellect and warms the heart. It is flowing from a movement that existed before time, beyond the intellect. The dimension of it all is recaptured in an international setting, evolving into pure art."
> —W. Henry Eccleston

There are subjects and ideas that lend themselves very well to poetry when I write, while other ideas definitely lend themselves to the visual art when I paint. Sometimes concepts and ideas flow that can easily be interpreted in poetry or paintings, and so the challenge is left to me to do both. Other times I think of loved ones who have touched my life and who my life has touched so profoundly in many meaningful ways, leaving lasting impressions. Those are memories most people just ignore and brush aside. Because of fear they never allow them to see the light of day. I reached beyond myself to put some thoughts forward in these pages. Those memories that still lingers on, some carved deep and etched within, while some just simply refuse to die or go away and chose to be cherished forever.
By: W. Henry Eccleston

W. Henry Eccleston was born in Jamaica West Indies in the parish of Trelawney. He was the third of eight children. He spent his early childhood and teen age years growing up in Trench Town, Western Kingston, the same community that nurtured the likes of Joe Higgs, Bob Marley, Alton Ellis, Authense Ellis, Delroy Wilson, and the many known musicians whom have pioneered Reggae music in that era between 1957 and 1974. He lends himself to the visual art and poetry and graduated from the Jamaica School of Art, now known as the Edna Manley School of the Visual and Performing Arts. Eccleston have been working, studying, painting, writing poetry, lecturing and traveling abroad now for over thirty-four years. He is co-host of the Midnight Ravers, an award winning radio program that is aired on alternate Fridays from midnight to 2:00 a.m. on WBAI 99.5 FM in New York.

By: Roger Steffens
Founding Edior, The Beat

ACKNOWLEDGEMENTS

First to my beautiful wife, Itine; son, Roshard; and daughter, Susan, who have been the glue that holds everything together. To my Mom, Josephine, and Dad, Alfred, who instill in me values.

To all my friends who help make this book possible: Leonard Stewart, Melvin Cunningham, Yvonne Walcott, Keith Pasquale, Joan Gilbert, Anthea McGibbon, Jacintha T. deFreitas, Fania Simon, Rondie Pottinger, Delroy Thompson, Antonia Marie Tapper and my editorial staff.

THIRTY YEARS IN BROOKLYN

The Vietnam War a dying ember.
Much bitter taste, the souls
whose bodies have come to waste.
The hippies' flower power,
children come to bloom.
New York, New York
the bosom,
five Boroughs suckle at her breast.
In Brooklyn, I have come to rest.

One highlight of my past
September 16, 1974, stood fast.
Arriving here from the Reggae land
this city gave new birth to my purpose.
Mayor Abe Beame succeeded John Lindsay
each with a new amended concession.
The city transit fare, thence 25 cents
free rides on holidays and Sundays
with transfer, whisk you across town.

Aroma from Nathan's hot dogs
filled the D train cabs from Stillwell Avenue
five miles stretch of boardwalk—beaches
filled with pleasure-seeking people
riding the Cyclone and (Wonder) Ferris wheel.
Water balloons pop under pressure
from spewing water gun surprises.
Memories, sweet memories
the chili on crusted hot dog buns.

New worlds open with summer sessions:
Pratt Institute and New York University.

Summer ends, fall leaves blow wantonly
adorning major highways and streets
with Prospect Park shedding
its lush green glory—now becoming gloomy.
Her botanical garden prepares.
She lays in seasonal slumber.
Fall frost gives way to winter snow
above her sleeping bed

The browning of the season
hisses with azure–manganese sky
cloaked in winter garb—of icicle needles
shielding naked bare bark trees
reflected lights dancing day and night along their spines.
The golden-hued city comes alive!
Brooklyn, New Yorkers—business as usual, continuously.

MUSIC OF THE SPHERE

Sometimes I'm up and traveling, spending
moments with old friends of long time passes.
As guest I'd been invited where pure souls
who are worthy are permitted and allowed to go.

I alighted from my mansion here on earth below
breaking through the barriers of this physical
universe that I grow so accustomed to.
I'd catapulted beyond energy, matter
space and time, looking back at mother earth
filled with her human kind.

Though my trip to Venus is still in this galaxy
I could not have alighted there in matter this earth
World vehicle fitted and placed me in
time, space, energy, and matter I'd defied
to gain the benefits worthy souls cannot be denied.

I arrived in a garden amid some ancient trees.
Sculptured were those garden paths with rows
of fragrant honey suckle leaves.
There stood my ancient friend from my distant past.
Rami Nuri, attired in a natural color robe, stood fast.

He greeted me in shared calmness and with a gentle smile.
Not a word was spoken nor exchanged there for a while.
With common understanding we commune as friends,
just two gentle souls meeting there once again.

We strolled along the garden path to his humble home
abode, there stood to greet us were his only son and wife.
We got dressed for supper in a humble dining room.

The repast was excellent with desert delicious at best.
I raised my head to say thank you without uttering
a single word, for there we communicated telepathically.

From there we move to a concert music hall.
Humbly Hugh and yet very bland.
He placed me in the first row right—next to the
cellist stand, and there he reached into a large case,
revealing his instrument, a Hugh bass fiddle he played
in the orchestral band.

I glanced across the stage to where the musicians
and string instruments of all description, displayed.
The conductor raised his left hand and with the
small white baton placed between his right fingers,
he pointed it at the musicians whose gazes became
as one, he flicked his wrists the orchestral sound began.

The sweet harmonizing stringed instruments
sound all crystallized as one, and there it was
like a celestial heavenly band.
I listened intently not through my ears
but as it were, through every fiber of my being
rejoiced to hear that heavenly harmonized band.

And soon began a solo part Rami commenced
to play, it was such music so divine, some sounds
I've never heard before, echoing throughout this
soul's inner being.
Then I reflect back on earth, if there was such a one
who could produce such sounds so pure with share?
Delight.

The only one there of his kind was Pablo Casals
who would have gladly joined with me and said,

W. Henry Eccleston

"I have never heard sounds so pure or of its kind"
The sound I heard transported me as it were in
The highest mansion of the sphere.
When the musician were done, the only three
left standing were Rami Nuri, this soul, and
the Blessed One.
They took me home again, to my mansion
made by spirit bare hands.

SIEVE TO PURIFY

Blessed One, the God worlds advancing.
The I-Cleve-to-Its-Heart Center.
A pleasure—workers in the mystic worlds
always looking forward, receiving.
Somehow it remains—you're planted, bloom there.
Need not say too much—of all the news that's good,
illusive—can't be held within your palm.
Getting closer brings eluding elevations
some years ago. Just be, all things well—the universe intended.

Go about your daily life—path will open, what spirit is willing.
How?—All I have done is wish to share a few with you.
God is real—Eck* is life.
Just be, and I am very pleased and will be with you always.
If the light and sound experience and see
day and night a farce and all the dreams
I've had—then will someone please, explain
the inner beings met, are real—with those so willing.

With a spiritual traveler—a dream, I had some while ago:
he took me in a shopping mall—stood at one end, observing
people as they pass by—shopping.
A lady came up, and arrogantly said, "Please,
how do I get into the inner mall" in which
many activities engage?
Pointing the way, she advances.
Minutes later returned, saying she can't find the entrance
where the traveler walked me through, minutes before.
After two attempts she came back, still not entered.

I realize that lesson the master teaches was for me.
Immediately, dawned—she could not enter, lacking purification.

W. Henry Eccleston

The illustration taught: this physical world in which we live,
should we not enter into highest experience?
Knowledge came—of someone grinding wheat
putting it in a sieve, separating the large particle—to be refined.
Only the fine grains—purified will go through;
the large particles never will.
Put the large ones back into the grinder.
Grind them smaller, perhaps they will.

Some Eckists** are like chunks of grain,
we wish to pass through, and be sieved.
We'll never pass until we're, grounded and refined.
The spirit of God alone shall—we'll gain entrance.
Seeker taught patience that day.

*Eck: The Audible Life Current.
** Eckist: Seekers, spreading the word of God

*SECRET MOMENTS ENJOYED

With engaging eyes, I latched on to her—
half way down—just below her belly button.
Our eyes made four—staring in each other's faces.
I knew what my thoughts were,
by the expression on her face—that of hers
different from mine—night from day.
I persist—then insisted to know
more about her—as if, by digging in her head—
trying to find out—what's in her thoughts—
all that's there—"you are a married man."
I meant nothing more, to her
For me—lustful pleasure, burning, deep desires
obliging me that Sunday.
She took me, for a visit—to her father's church.

W. Henry Eccleston

SECRET MOMENTS ENJOYED

Engaged eyes, latched on the Virgo's pendant
hung to the bottom of her chain around her neck
followed her cleavage half-way down—
just below the belly button.
Our eyes made four, as we stared piercingly with glazed eyes.
I knew my thoughts, twirled inside my head.
Expression on her face—that of hers differs from mine—
as Jupiter's freezing temperature stretches far from Mars.
I persist—then insist to know
more about her—as if, by digging in her head
trying to define, liked thoughts—just what lies in her mind.
All that's there is "you are a married man."
For me—lustful pleasures, burning desires; deep inside my head
pent up like wild fire, blazing to consummate.
I meant nothing that way—to her.
One other thing—she obliged me, three full hours
as we sit in my directors chairs—two talking heads
pounding away, comparing life's philosophies.
So much familiarity—O! The similarities!
In thoughts we were like pure energy, emanating from the sun
giving warmth to earth's fertile longevity
with intellect intact—I chauffeured her home that day.

THREAT OF THE BIG ONE

Longer than I've lived my single life of twenty-six years.
One year before—I know her well enough.
It's thirty years since we said I do.
We shared a wonderful life raising a family.
In her Jacuzzi she made the dreadful discovery.
She shouted my name in a different kind of way
that hastens my steps to her screams.
"Feel this," she hastily said.
A lump the size of the fleshy side of my thumb.
"It burns like fire—the heat is spreading,
creating a long lasting hot sensation."

MORTALS MANSION

Descended
standing, encased in my mansion walls
the day, I, Soul, greatly fall.
Stranger I've become
not being able to travel to and from
neither the inner nor outer universe.
That's the day I, Soul Encased,
become mortal man.

Nothing seems to mirror of former time
when—I knew no bounds or end.
Omnipresence, omniscience, and omnipotence—
my will. Gone are the *is-ness* days
where Truth and Love to give were my desire.
Now I move about, encased in human shell
with five senses and faculties to coordinate.
I learn to manipulate this course matter, world
having much to do in time
gaining earthly knowledge and wealth.

A wanderer I have become these days
decked out with five passion seeds:
vanity, anger, lust, attachment, and greed.
Seeking to regain blessings in isolation
I drink in loneliness, joy through human understanding.

This tainted role, I began to play
stockpiling earthly goods, manipulating
my fellow beings, creatures, minerals, and plant life too
ranting, raving, and causing destruction
creating deceptive delusions along my path.

At the closing end of day when all work is done
old and feeble I've become
gazing through the windows of my mansion walls
at my exploitation stacks of hoarded earthly wealth.
The five passions have helped me gain
I can't exchange them then—for happiness nor peace.

Not one earthly thing there is to show
of the kindness I have done.
Wretched man that I become
a choice to do it all again
I'd thirst for wisdom, then
once more for Truth and Love.

TRENCH TOWN REMINISCENCE

South West of Kingston is Trench Town—
I love to reminisce!
Thinking of the life once lived
now memories frozen in thought,
where some warriors, the rough, the tough
Rude Boys and Girls in graves now lay,
the souls who could have lived,
to fulfill their destined role.
Blinded by infantile darkness
fashioned without hope,
they could see no farther than,
a poverty-stricken, dull world.

Memories linger still
carved deep and etched within.
The innocent, through no fault of theirs
gunned down in their prime.
Starving children crying
groaning from painful hunger.
Much is the disdain from the upper strata
of society; suffrage within a lesser cast.
Fertile were our peoples' minds, having not
The wherewithal; coming to maturity -
counted that for something.
We would plot a path in life,
flowing deep from within our rustic, multi-cultural souls.

I sometimes think in wonder,
how swiftly our years come and go,
having sat to ponder, under the tree of guanga,
or up high, between ackee tree branches,
where the cool breeze blow

soft winds passing,
whistling among the leaves.
There, where the orange red
closed fruit in clusters swayed,
became fit to open, then to pick.

Like a handful of carbon nuggets human-
gems, scattered throughout our cultured turf
polished beyond our darkened will.

Through faith, some "Rudies" have seen the light
risen through slum's suppression.
Spiritual attainment in sight
with consciousness gleaned, molded to substance,
like diamonds in the rough.
Larger than religion, bigger than life's oppression
the *Is-ness* of all things, cause and effect
overcoming adversities, principles universal.
All nations, classes, castes and creeds come to reap
gleaning of our virtues and culture at will.
Trench Town! Trench Town! Trench Town!
O how I love to reminisce
in heightened praise.

WEST KINGSTON GHETTO TROUBLES

Ghetto People, Ghetto People! Ghettoooo,
Hear this roll call, of our sinful—karmic names.
What crimes have we committed?
Coronation Market by Darling Street,
does it really matter Ghetto Souls at their feet,
scourged by majority in society?
Used by poly-trick-sans
last to reap the bounties IMF issues them as loans
packaged skillfully with our scornful groans.
Poly-tricksters flaunting with their bellies full
acquired affluent tastes—the Ghettoooes,
while we cry of human suffrage—from hunger pains.

Congregating in a tenement yard—smoking herb,
industrious Rasta women knitting caps and gowns,
under tamarind tree. Brethren strumming their guitars,
harmonizing in happiness, the ushering of new sounds.
Illallu and fish, our staple diet
down at Greenwich Farm Bay, casting our nets,
running boat in a kitchen—children must eat.
Whatever ration scuffled provided us a treat.

New hope peeping through the dawn of day.
Family must provide nursing the hurt, the bleeding deep inside.
Not much skill to offer, employment looking bleak,
nothing for the taking—there's no faking, in Coubourn Pen.
Selling coolie plums, freshly picked each day,
some sit on gully wall, others race board horses,
gutter water as the race track—we hustle a wager's call.

Disenfranchisement rattles our brain

inventing ways how we would get around.
Street smarts, no takers—empty shells remain.
When pipe line lack—no water flowing.
Ignorance our teacher, poverty and pain our best friends—again?
Ghettoooes- devastation- desolation—isolation,
Denham Town Police Station—prison over Bumper Hall,
May Pen Cemetery, Spanish Town Road,
JAH! Our solace,
O! Shelter our wretched, naked souls again?

MISSING YOU

Moments pass
while I live my life
filling each seconds with virtues come my way
stacking the minutes, multiplying into days
Seven days in counting. Oh how the moments swiftly passed
loaded with things to do, that I have done.
And yet, though quite accomplished
no guilt trip rests on me.
For I have done—my, what things to do "successfully"
I'm, somehow—feeling empty deep inside
without you being here.
If you were, my moments of stockpiling things to do
your presence would be among the moments,
seconds, and in my every day
while these two weeks have passed.

MISSING YOU

Moments pass
while I live my life
filling each seconds with virtues.
Stacking minutes, multiplying into days
seven days in counting,
Oh! How the moments swiftly fly away.

Without you being here,
I'm empty deep inside.
If you were numbered among things to be done
your happiness would be my priority
in my every day
appreciation of your virtue then.

CLARITY OF VISION

Sometimes I sit with gazing eyes,
just looking out in space.
Perhaps there's something else to see.
Maybe I'll find what others claim to see,
and dub creativity?
Why should I be bothered
with the abstract you appreciate,
in a funny looking scenic picture,
or in some silly frame?

I call a spade a spade.
That is how I was trained to be.
Why should I care what you see,
if to me, a leaf is a leaf, and a tree a tree!?
Portrait and traditional painting is enough for me.
In my vision, appreciation is complete,
a pebble is a pebble and a rose is just a simple rose.

FRESH FACE

With my gazing eyes
I see her piercing eyes.
I glance upon your face,
fresh and radiating,
relating untold stories.
"What have you applied to your face?" I hinted.
She sighed, then revealed
masked compact substances—
Silky, shiny substances
"You applied Fresh Face?"
Left me so bewildered.
A pinch of this, a spot of that
a drop of this,
a dust of you know what?,
A swab of this, a brush of that
and heaven knows
what else you've got?

W. Henry Eccleston

ARE YOU AWARE?

Are you aware of the hurt I fear?
You there, sitting in your easy chair!
Do you feel love's burning desires
that sets my aching bones on fire?
Is it your thoughts, I feel my dear,
or is it my own mirage, I fear?

You camouflage in deep facade
your memories, your thoughts.
You do not wish to bring alive
the emotions you shield with logics
then, with care I fear.

Depressed thoughts.
Repressed. Suppressed!
Is self denial worse than karma or sin?
Then, let your thoughts come alive!
Give them wings to soar, and then fly
never allowing—die, die, and die!

DO YOU FEEL THE HURT

Just to sit and gaze at you:
do you know the hurt it brings?
The hurt I feel, thinking of your love
wishing it will somehow heal,
through my envisioned sensual appeal?

In endless thoughts, I walk away
surviving memories of you every day.
But soon after, it's back again
playing games,
bringing me deeper into despair.

Without you standing there
I can only watch through my memory's eyes.
Dancing silhouettes to my deep despair,
my broken heart now torn apart
from memories of that which I bore no fault.

For months on end, I paint your portraits
with hopes that the fiery thoughts,
of you will come to a screeching end.
Knowing all along, the fears and doubts
wedges heavily in my head.

Flowing from the inner source
I try to stop the blazing force.
Through my inner being
the flow of memories comes rushing.
I have no choice but to surrender all,
to the tick tock, tick tock,
ticking, ticking to the inner clock.

W. Henry Eccleston

THE HOUSE IN WHICH WE DWELL

The house in which we dwell
as visitors passing through,
is souls' precious gift
given so freely without penalty.
The Creator of this spark
gives room on board for souls who seek to come
aboard and sought out their heavy load,
while gaining experiences.

Builds mansion, with invisible hands
fitted them well, with all the fine necessities
of glamour and all precious amenities.
The brain and the five senses as the main frame,
to explain all abstractions.
With hands and feet to move about, eyes, ears, mouth,
all other body parts—lending great support
with senses to coordinate through wisdom.
Knowledge, we expedite growth
moving about while gaining experiences.

Through the years as marines we sail
the earth and soar throughout its vast
uncharted universes—gliding, floats above like eagles,
flying on thin air. Others walk about as penguins
Plop, plop; plopping on thin granite rocks gathering experiences.

We tell tales of long ago
through history we have left behind
linking our every day while we work,
sleep, eat, have fun at play.
With drubs of dreams, we create philosophies
of Wisdom and great Knowledge

spinning webs in Spirituality, coupling human discussions,.
Religion and religious right wings keep on
unfolding we plot and make our way,
improving minds, and making new concessions of
past actions unfolding memories so controlling.

There's only one aim in life, trying to define—
few will find the true fated reality.
Sailing the cosmic sea of time,
breaking barriers going behind
where mortals, shall never trod or touch.
Nothing in this vast universe
can ever match with worth
the joys and visions there,
where we souls have often been
crossing borders willingly—sometimes unknown.

Understanding mortals—
never deemed resolved.
What is in its scheme of things!
In scope, they understand with five senses,
wisdom gained only with their minds;
hands and feet mull, prod about endlessly.
Cycles upon cycles, they keep transforming again,
entering life's beginning—not knowing
they are restarting something
they knew ever so long ago.

Chosen few understand the pace they're traveling
hastening through the span of time
reaching destinations, earning gifts left so long ago,
embarking upon their human journey
all one family traveling in different groups
learning Truth much to our amazement -
and from the discontented forces seldom understood.

W. Henry Eccleston

How do they case the span of time?
Chasing ideologies, endless atrocities,
conforming to earthly ideas burning
deep down in their hearts consuming
brimstone and fire, not knowing of what they're seeking.
What manner of man is this, they come calling?
Just because they found a gifted one so willing
who trusted daring, blazing fire wrapped up in his bones?
Hard time enduring, honesty deep inside
letting this world know what he had endured.
Took few gifted friends—men and women drifted about
following his shadow hoping to enlighten
whoever will may come—be part of the team.
Vaguely remembering times, of long so long ago?

What tragedy befalls mortal man?
Make mockery of the universal plan—playing God?
Pretend he is doing it a favor,
trying to save something they think is lost,
but could never have been: soul of which I am speaking
could never have been lost!
In the predicament man find himself to be
playing God is nothing but a cop-out
for he does not need mortals' help.
The only way man can truly help—simply empty him
Of himself then, just (be).
The creator of this great universe may find grace
and favor in his eyes, uses him as a channel sacrifice.

To be used thence is not even using mortal man.
God has used the reaction of himself at will.
The spark he induces, placing it in a house,
the Souls mansion on earth.
How then, can the made become the maker?

Soul alone will endure its journey home, again
gathering its experiences and long moved on
while man's body, mind, hands, feet, brain, and all its
Faculties will not be needed any more, will dissolve in oblivion
Whence it came—until time permits its use
To hosts some new visitor, Souls again ... and again.

* *Dedicated to Inner Spirits so pure.*

W. Henry Eccleston

CONVICTED, IF FOUND GUILTY

You took me on charged to your inner forces
I then pleaded my cause with mine.
Though from a human point of view
the effects look grim, and mighty sad.
They hoarded me in a courtroom
so placid, and yet so grand.
The walls were freshly painted
blood red and French splash navy blue.
Much to my surprise, I gazed upon the
ground on which I stand.
Œ Taw's nowhere else than in the Palm
of God's great and mighty hands.

I heard the voice say,
"What is your name? I have needed to pull your files."
By the time I thought of what to say
a neat little filing cabinet was placed by my side.
A thumb and an index finger reached out,
opened it next to me.
And to my amazement
guess what was my surprise?
All the jokes that we had ever shared
were placed there by my side.
Every breath I had ever breathed in your presence
from the day we first met.
displayed right there before me.

Man that I am! How I began to fret.
Then for a brief moment
I stood there thinking to myself.
Thoughts of years gone by
the great friends that I had met.

In my vision, stood the high and the mighty
the lowly, and the poor,
the rich man, the affluent,
the beggars, and the thieves.
There were countless people
whom I had only met with
just a simple gaze.

From where I stand there, in God's hands
no status, casts, class, nor creed bare any significance.
For there, all that really matters was purity
adorned in Holy love.
I then reflected upon the case on which I had
at hand; a ringing sound pierced through my ears
like a rumbling voice heard, a charge sent deep to my Soul.
"On what charges, are you brought here"?
"I am charged for being too graphic!
By my closest friends so pure,
"What selfish gestures, had you induced?"
"None that I can think of, not then, not now."
Selflessness was my only friend
that day, the whole way, through.

Unselfish Love was my forte
and that I stand to give.
My closest friend said, "What are
you getting for yourself?" and this
was my reply. "Nothing that I can think of
For, I am here to give and not to receive!"
"I swear!"
"No need to swear, for I can see in your heart.
I was there on that day, in your selfless company."
"I am not here to ask you for sympathy, nor empathy,
For if I'm found guilty; then mitigate my just reward."

W. Henry Eccleston

The voice replied, "I am searching for
the selfishness that you intend, and
indeed I have found none".
"All, I found you guilty of is giving from your bounties
and questioning
The precious gifts that, I, God, so freely gave."
"I found that your only wish was, to furnish others with gifts.

One piece of advice.
Some gifts in life are better left alone
if not presented to you.
For there is no greater gift
than that which springs purely from the soul.
Manifesting love in this physical universe
triggers human emotion.
Of the mind world, is by far a lesser love
than what is expressed from the Soul?
True love from the Soul, is all I intended
through you my vessel
on such a great and blissful day."

Never speak about the gifts you give.
Go forth only—and spread my work.
For any day, I find you again
standing in my courts
If I find you in guilty
You'll be the worthless Soul.
I'll be forced to throw the book at you,
and you will neither be hers, nor my friend."

MY TWIN FLAME

Mere mortals shall not understand,
The love I bear for you at hand.
Your love so pure, yet so divine
sometimes tend to blow my mind.

We cross paths, you claim my heart.
Twin flame, our fire is blazing!
Most lives have passed; Oh! So fast
without ever engaging!

I'm crossing paths with my twin flame.
I'll make damn sure the best is gain.
And yes, it's without failing
the result will be of fame.

With most trust-filled relationships,
rewards in my earthly life.
I have known love's imprints before
but never experienced one so pure.

RED FIELD OF DREAMS

Red Field of Dreams keeps on—
bleeding into life.
The thing which holds our every being,
controlling, oh so slight,
I can hardly recognize it.
Even though it's tsunamis, growing tidal waves are moving,
hastening to their swelling, bellowing end.

There, it comes again in its repetitive cloning patterns,
churning again and again, Ever repeating its present -
discontent! If only I know the answer to this puzzle
or the pressing question to the answers they demand?

Time marches onward throughout every civilization
creating discontent; which mortal being can capture
the soul of Time and send it back to God?
What!—You do not realize
that even time is Soul, encased in its shell
as does your red field of dreams?

Seems every move I make
is under the control of the mind.
As if it is an illusion burning
within confusion, deep, deep inside, while
Red Field of Dreams just keeps on bleeding,
Ever flowing with bleak discontent.
Like ancient rivers once flowing
through the Great Sahara Desert
now changed in courses …
bursting their banks
as the Mighty Mississippi River,
or the great Hudson Valley Stream.

The rain clouds move so swiftly
reacting, creating their offspring—lightning
which sometimes resonate as thunder bolts.
Tornados swirling like music playing
dancing through the elements of time
all caressed by the Red Field of Dreams

I was there in the land of Mo.
There time flew
within its own limitations
Adding confusion
creating its own illusive bag of tricks
I have watched men being fooled

At times, I, to other lacking souls, hinted
this or that I dream to know.
On the Red Field of Dreams
there were souls stuck in time
going round and round
chasing their illusive visions in redundancy.
My focused kindness keeps moving in Red Field of Dreams
through time.

I remember when Time was born -
or before, when Time was just a thought
a desire locked deep inside of me.
Her incarnation as a baby wedged in limitation.
It too was just a dream waiting for its
mirthful purpose to be born.

I watched my fellow beings that were pure souls
there and then; take unto themselves to dwell
in the mortal mansions built for them.

W. Henry Eccleston

They slowed themselves down, adjusting and
waiting on time to tell them when,
how to move and go about, when to sit,
when to stand, when to talk, how to plan.

Some Holy books in soundness quote Solomon.
He said, "A time to live and a time to die."
Solomon becomes just a man, sitting,
waiting as soul on time again, and again.
Do you not know who you were before time?
Before you became a unit encased in its shell?

Why then should I, being Soul, surrender
myself to Time?
With her tenderness, Time she induces,
I have seen Her hold great souls,
making mere mortals out of them.
It seems, they have no hope nor memory,
for they have long ago
lost there soul's identity to Time who was once a baby.

It is amazing how Souls allow themselves to become
just mortal, surrendering themselves to time's passion,
relinquishing all to their infant sister Space, daughter.
Suns, moons, stars, and galaxies all were created for Time.
At the birth of Time, the entire inner universe
rejoiced, showering her below in the parallel
world with precious gifts; so I had to expand
space to contain them for her, and yes! Her Gifts were aplenty.
Energy was needed to keep them all in place.

New worlds, galaxies, planets
and oceans of stars like us, still are spark of God.
Yes! Time is but a spark of God. She too is soul.
So is Space and Energy—all are equal too, as you and me.

Equipped with knowledge and wisdom serving; inner universes
Time like us re-incarnates, on the wheel of life for millenniums,
and everything moving in this Red Field of Dreams.

There in the higher inner planes energy fields, where
there were great souls like Captain Kirk, Scotty,
and Mr. Spock with their mother loads.
Now all are trapped between times!
Space and energies here below,
now becoming mortal beings.
Those were once ancient mariners exploring
inner universes, quasars, and galaxies.
All now trapped, becoming
mortals, serving Time, but for a while.
They have long forgotten the Red Field of Dreams
And when their younger sister Space
was created, until they remember their identity, being souls,
they will all be trapped servants of time repetitively.

Only in the Red Field of Dreams—until we recognized erudition,
serving each other's souls, as equal sparks; emanating pure Holy love
to adjust our conditions—will we have access.
The Dream Weaver shall disconnect us
from the webbed womb of mother time.

Once again,
we will become: coworkers—emancipated mariners, explorers,
Exploring inner galaxies,—keepers of the inner flames beyond time
Her gifts of space expansion, of energy, suns, moons
stars, planets, earth, external galaxies, and parallel universes.

W. Henry Eccleston

BIRTHRIGHT

Push the pencil swiftly against the paper.
Sketch it, paint it, write it, create it—be it!
Take charge—the universe is under your control.
It bears your reserve—own it.
The ether holds your potency.
Claim it!
Intellectual properties—yours—glean it.
Work as though you are God—pure Soul.
Like beings speaking—working through you,
letting potent energies flow.
Talk not too much about it—lack is a curse.
What purity inner forces provide, they hold for you.
Why renege? Fear not. Let it flow from within,
in the element. -
Feelings of dissatisfaction come and go,
all within the passing of time.
Let not any one mood overwhelm you
nor monopolize your abilities to advance.
Persist. Insist.
Comes your way—go through the experiences.
Persist, process—create longevity.
Repelling disappointment, I Have arrived,
claiming my birthright!

BEYOND MIND OVER MATTER

Clouded mind wrapped with pent-up
feelings deep inside, piercing like needles,
penetrating every fiber of my being.
Present discontent affecting my dreadlocks—
which come to stand on end,
Like antennas receiving signals everywhere

On razors edge, I stand,
cry out—a scream!
Echoes! Of my darkest night heard
from Thirteenth Street. Up a tank
sounded through to First Street, and
across May Pen Cemetery,
attracting voices, bombarding,
marching like soldiers
giving orders, waiting for the subjects
to follow their commands.
Like guard dogs,
the watchmen guard my gate,
relinquishing not to foreign forces
seeking to penetrate

Ticking clock, tick tock, tick ticking,
and time matters not.
On the cliff of my mind where I stand,
viewing and watching a creative thought,
waiting to be born,
interpret to my will
in a poem, a painting, or a song.
There, where time stood still,
I stepped beyond Earth matter world.
Reap the gifts wedged deep in my mind
between the light and sound.

W. Henry Eccleston

YOU LOVING ME FOR ME

Mom and dad created me,
swear I am fair within their eyes.
Should some suitor come along, giving the same reply?
Should he not make a new entry, singing a brand-new song?
Something, I can appreciate—willing to share; then go along.

It takes more than just sucking up to win my heart.
No mister nice guy act, nor patronizing will attract.
Neither his talking head, nor convincing tongue, show differently.
Begging, bird call chasing, pleading, nor cooing will attract.

Is it my permission, or convincing approval, desired for me to tug along?
Nothing further from the truth—this amount of kissing up brings contempt.
Let me buy her precious jewelry, wine and dine—in fancy restaurants,
hoping to compensate convincingly—not even this will approve.

One simply little feat—loving me for me.
There, sharing and enjoying me for me.
Then we'll get along.
No amount of pushing, prodding—merely making me feel loved
and wanted by you, as me, for me:
this will pull the best of me.

I, then, will accept you, as you, for you—your personality.
This alone will retain your individuality. Relinquish not for me.
Firmly be, in whatever you do—your approach; demand and needs.
Reach out, and then touch—I'll reach out touching—relationships
to prolong.

VIRGIN'S BIRTH

Foreign substance,
substance foreign,
grew inside his exposed wife's womb.
All poets conferred and writers wrote about it.
None ever deemed it fit
to demonstrate the reasons
beyond neither cause nor effect.

What and why the effect affected by the cause
or the cause that caused the cause to affect
foreign substance.
Substance foreign
grew in his exposed wife's womb.
History said, he did not put it there.
It did.
    Amen

DIVINE MENTOR

In this corporate world I stand!
Casing the span of time,
looking to my Divine Mentor,
having placed my life in his care,
being tailor-made by him
to custom fit my ways,
fashioned to the precepts of his will.

Design me with stamina—
there are many more mountains to climb;
valley, streams, and rivers to cross;
and cold weathers to endure.
Trials mounting—I, being dissolved,
create within the light and sound,
adjusting to new resolve.
Cause has placed me here.
I am in It—the divine sphere!

MANKIND AND HIS RACE

Spend no time blaming the man
for what grinder he puts us through.
I do not know what divine deeds we have done,
deserving of this strange reward.
They inflict a charted assigned roll,
an act of faith that has brought us forces,
two races colliding together. Starting at the starter's block.
Herded, then penned, a subjugated stock.
Duly inflicted pain, by nature, we are pushing back,
such an uneven feat, racing relentlessly.

The earth bears our resourceful substance.
He—the nudge for technology.
And I, for fertile resources and creativity.
He stands in greater fame, fortune, and power.
I—the disenfranchised, starving race,
grinding daily under his watch,
struggling endlessly to make ends meet.
Which of us is the more accomplished?
He, being affluently wealthy—I, being wretchedly poor?
What measure defines merit, determine which is best?
None can stand alone; partial is incomplete.

This universe sets in motion harmony between us two.
What gifts she's justly granted,
given freely for us all to glean.
Sometimes she does a cleansing, to reset in harmony
man's subjective will, deemed otherwise.
Go against in chaos of Earth's choosing,
conditioning the minds to ideas deemed fit
in circumstances we defined ourselves.
Coming in, going out, like waves on turquoise sea.

W. Henry Eccleston

Purpose to define, that fits the moods we are in.
Poverty, pain, and suffering be the humble fortress
of what hides the doorway of truth from view.
Of those keeping company with illusions,
they are the friends of deadly, destructive vices,
blocking the highway of truth, compassion, and peace,
though you stockpile, hoarding endlessly,
claiming even that which is under the lesser feet.
What will be your purpose thence?
When the gleaning stocks complete
or you have run your course?

The greatest feat mankind has attained—
his sons have touched the moon,
sharing with his fellow beings endless galaxies.
America, America—USA your eagled eyes—
we raise our hats and sing you praise.
Our God has made you the first,
created jazz, deep in the belly of Mardi gras plain
dark—creates the music, through Souls wounded bodies
who have lived the pain, against all enduring odds?
Your uncommon ways to treat us—
stockpiling your reserve and generating logs
illegally—gathering imprints of your children's intent.
Your stock is not to feed us, while hoarding us as guest.

Are the affluent able to hear the voice of God?
Shadowed by greed, subjugating his fellow clan.
Or are the needy sufferers any closer?
Brooding, nursing poverty in pain,
giving neither advantage, they play a reverse role,
for none have really attained the chosen plane.
Reversed roll we will ever play, at the end of days,
on and on until—understanding the process, subtle plan
by a greater force, setting motion—in great disguise,
waiting endlessly through ages, for our changes at will.

AWESOME LOVERS' RETREAT

Longer than I have lived my single life—
one year after, knowing her somehow—
the winter month of December 13
in warm consummation,
birthing a wonderful life, sprouting with changes
grinning; and rivaling each other's space
ruffled the changing seasons bringing surprises.
Summer sizzle, winter feast sparkled delight,
arrival trilling our true test at best.

Two siblings, a daughter and a son, glorifying life
raising them through the years, in thoughts
provoke thinking, that they're raising us.
Each grows accustomed to do's and don'ts,
responding at will, to their claimed spaces.
Friday night things become filled with weekend
pleasure-filled delight ... sucking up to each moment
wringing them dry, equally. The weekdays equate
learned much, communicate with pride,
what joy fulfilled.
Just let me be. I am aware of the recycling pile
racing, testing ways to handle free will and trial
with farce ways enlisted a tested deal.

Loosing hearts true desire, to gain flirtation fire
quenching thirsty emotions—burning bright.
The ideal a clue, for not straying but holds firm.
Together consider being boxed in—holding to sway
forces that form the glue. Mother and daughter
work in harmony, not rivaling in each other's face.
Everything's right for you and yours.
Kisses with shades of love while joy overflows.

W. Henry Eccleston

Consider our son's structured warm appeal, words
to impress upon, enticing some suitor who strolls along,
blending in as one with a thoughtful plan.
Needing him somehow, come closer. I'll transform
her. I'll reform you, sweet lady, clasping hands tightly
together, waiting to say, "I do."
Whatever comes, replace immaturity with maturity.
Live for privacy. He evades precious gaming moments,
opportunities she will gladly share, a feast of
her will and passion well intent

Privilege ferment, making chase in life
capable—feeling exercise pain that recedes.
Suffice surfer, the big wave crashes.
You think and then conquer the height,
foaming tower of emotion,
like water rolling, pushes surfing delight.
What happiness subsides, adrenaline rush more fun!
I'm not saying you cannot be ousted,
trying time implode what thoughtfulness explode,
pawns to gain, the enlightened will of others
rushing, juxtaposing to the top,
blazing flames, in arms closed fists unclenched.

TYPICAL GHETTO LIVITY

(I)

Knowing, that we are not lazy,
having brain tissues, and muscles, to bare
the willingness for work.
How do we get in with the grinding source?
Much negative and bigotry, red tape to cut
affluently wealthy, poverty a-plenty.
We know, we're stocked in lack, with no food to glean,
not even to stretch, filling our children's need.
On hungry bellies, we try to school them,
wishing, they could get the education we never had.
"Water more than flour," we'd always say.
No work—four days left in the week.

Devastatingly broke, it is shaping up to be
no money in our pockets as yes, we ah fret.
Without any jobs, what will we do?
Seeing others—the better, fortunate
living easier. Elsewhere, barely carving out
a crumb of bread to feed their families—
them we call the have-haves, and the haves,
for me, *haaaa!*—They call me the have-not.
What's there that makes it so? we ask ourselves.
Class, cast, and creed filter down from
the upper echelon of society, favoring the chosen,
depending on whose party you're in.

Back in the yard, Ms. Tense, miserable as hell—
two children, common-law husband hustling as well
to make ends meet—what can we say of that?
Knowing—somewhere there is affluence, in plenty,

W. Henry Eccleston

with much developments on the outskirt of town.
Cold supper shops, down West Road.
Mr. Pilot, running picka-pow and chipping
blocks of ice to quench the neighborhood thirst.
Sang-o over Third Street, on Fridays frying salt dog
and fresh fish, preparing for the weekend—all night. -
Fiesta and bingo ganja binge,
Big Hand over First Street with feh him, gambling den,
throwing bone dice and playing cards, almost every night.
Rude boys hang out in tenements yards.
Some played dominoes while shooting off their mouths.
Others, peddling ganga spliff and smoking wefer joints.
Mis-a P., blind as hell—selling share ice, making a living as well

(II)

There were some talented girls and boys,
champions within our town,
remembered still the afternoons.
The games our club, Boys Town, had played.
Mentors taught indoor games of children choosing.
While some sit on the grandstand benches,
other youths perch on whitewash fencing wall.
Some watched from the sidelines in the grass
or illegally sat on some fixed cricket boundary stone
with glazed eyes on the game in progress.
Scorekeepers at their desks, scoring play by play.
Little helpers climbed the scoring rack and registered
the last runs

Bunny, the peanut vendor with stocks of cashews
and chewing gum stacked up in his little tray,
carved out a livelihood, seeking a better way.
What an awesome, graceful sight to have seen
some cricketers, precision bats men at play:

Collie Smith, Pulus, Irving Stanley, and Victor Fray.
Sunny Levy, Cleveland Richards,
Sir Frank Worrell, or even Barger Ray.
Still, when it came to soccer—dribbling on the field
some exhibition pickup matches or even major league
like the mighty Pale, none could outshine our players—
Les or Carl Brown (the brothers Subaru) Darkens
Jonnie Cool, Œdago Gordon, Noel, and Larry Wint or not
necessary the Largie boys. How shall I forget the goalkeeper in
the net? ŒRespic Dragon Morgan, simply was the best.
With National pride at heart, we put up front the best.
Our primed athletes, eight of them one season, played
at their greatest, representing our Island through test
within the National Stadium walls,
on the cricket field, at Sabina Park, or sometimes
in competition matches on some foreign soil.

(III)

With not many skills to offer,
much raw talent lay to waste.
Gifted youth blend their voices
with groups, or sometime on their own.
Music seems to have been a vehicle,
which we could ride on, right out of town.
There were gifted ones, deemed it fit,
seeking wailing Joe Higgs's advice in music,
lessons from First Street to Fourteen Street.
Federal Gardens too—Concrete Jungle or
nooks and crannies in some other parts of
town. Shining stars—musicians, gifted.
They had become the rhythm masters
of those days. Taking the movements,
rhythm of the people, in creative ways,
shaping songs—events of the day as news

W. Henry Eccleston

from that period in time.

Molded it into music—with input from the
lesser to the greatest of us all, who some
time sat or stood, just listening, while the
artists sang and harmonized in the Kasbah.
Musicians developed their music, shaped it
into Mento, Ska, Rock Steady, and Reggae.
They in an off-based way, creating true forms
sound systems throughout the West, the East,
the North, and the South—blast new sounds,
echoing everywhere: Alton Ellis, Hopeton Lewis,
Wailing Wailers, the one love geniuses' Bunny
Livingston, Peter Tosh, Bob Marley, and Ken Booth;
Laurel Akins, Beverley Kelso, Cherry Green, Joey and
Andy, Orthense Ellis, Delroy Wilson, Stranger Cole,
with Wailing Soul; and many more.
When opportunity knocks,
Sigree Wesley, winner of the Veer John all-island
competition one year—coo, coo, cooing, drum,
drum, drumming,—check-check-checking, strum-
strum-strumming. Musicians tuning guitars
created their music to a cacophony of new sounds

(IV)

Mrs. Wesley, the milk lady, made her round once a week,
a new route every day, except Saturdays,
Sabbath day.
The fish man and his hand cart, with iced-down fish,
shouting through the streets "Fresh fish.
Fresh, fresh, fresh fish, fresh, fish."
The bread man from up a Purity Bakery
with his mule and cart, peddling his loafs
through our winding streets and lanes.

Ishmael—the coconut vender, on Sunday mornings,
Chop-chop-chop-chop-chopping—
selling fresh jelly coconut, in his two mule and dray cart,
peddling for a living. Hagglers, by
any means necessary, to feed a family,
buy and sell whatever provisions they
can purchase from the country folks,
coming in from rural parishes on market trucks
to sell and unlade their provision and wares.
Grandma Christie found something to do,
making and wiring black dolls, a popular
collector's item for the tourism trade
down at Craft Market, bottom of King Street,
beside Victoria's Pair

Religious organization giving out free food
in exchange if you would listen to their good news.
Upper West Road, close to Clock Tower on Eighth Street,
or in Church Lane, Capo the carver and many anointed elders,
Mothers and Pucko Mania's Captains dancing,
wheeling and singing, beating their drums,
chopped off a ram goat's head, drank its blood with rum
as a sacrament, working up a trance while venting
their woes, tuning in on the inner world.
Drawing strength to enter another day.

Those Rastafarian Brethren and Nyiabinghi women
light a bond fire, sing, and chant while beating
their funda drums to the tune of a call, for their
"Back to Africa" Rastafarian redemption songs.
Thursday was the government soup kitchen day,
a treat for some old folks in neighborhood yards:
who carried a food ration pass to get lunch that day?
Third Street and West Road or up at Seventh Street
were the Branch Yards. There, politicians offer their

blessings of empty promises—void of any substantial solution, year after year—decades after decades, we saw deterioration hover, all over the place, while the people still hoping—all in one cycle, making our neighborhood work.

NATTY BONGO SPEAKS

(I)

Human ideologies
messed up societies
coupled with brutality,
force and Power.
Having led its citizens astray
roping Natty Bongo to follow
from the Source, full original way.
How many lifetimes will it have to take
showing Mankind he has missed the path
to the error of his wanton ways?
Those further down the pike line
deceptive road, beckoning for all others
to join their smiling, swaying wrath.
Me nah go dah way de at all, Rasta say.
We nah go down de at all Rasta say.

(II)

You took me from my land
of golden sun shiny savannahs
far across the mighty ocean—wavy seas—
to work the hell out of me, all day
without pay, with sweat and blood running
down, building your land you took from
another, through a deceptive way,
leading me down the darkened path
of your adapted religious ways.

Not even stopping long enough to see
if that's the way to go, for me to go we

W. Henry Eccleston

mustn't go, and not even you know the
way. Thinking, convincingly that that's
the path to go, following that which you
place on a stick, convincing us all to go.
Just leave me alone ... alone! Stop planning
your deceptions and allow me to make
my way through my gate. I must go—me
must go—We nah go dah way deh at all with
you Rasta nah go dah way deh at all at all.

(III)
We rest our laurels
on human knowledge
coupled with emotions,
leading the game,
thinking thoughts that
that's the way to truth,
happiness, and peace.
Will we bear true to the light?
When will we then turn around?
Relinquishing the thoughts we hold,
there are those who walked away,
backtracking from the herd,
hoping then that they will find
the source repelling the sway
in the red, gold, and green. Rasta say me
Nah go dah way deh at all—Rasta says—me
Nah go dah way de at all! An a Africa me
Bound fah, you nah go sway me a-t all a-t all

PURPOSE

Though harsh it may be
purpose to fulfill
a God of love—
equates a God of dislike.

Not withstanding neutrality
in this world of greatest opposites:
darkness to a twilight night
morning, noon—and evening light..

At times—when I am awake
sleep will find me so opposed
to reasoning—fathoms unknown.
But then in time
I will know.

When I fulfill my desired course
of this my destined role
purpose then, my will fulfilled
mission that is complete at will
captured a beginning at my end.

NOT WITH MY EYES

Not with my eyes
I gaze at you
filling my heart with content.

Your perfume I smell
knowing it is only in my head.
My heart leaps for joy
whenever I think of your name.

Though you are miles away
distance makes no difference.
Having the need, I am with you
while in body you are not near.

Your image in my thought palace
in purity, on my mind's screen
does bring joys—content

FRYING FISH ROUND A CANARSIE

"Come! Let me give you some money."
"You can buy some fried fish, later in the today."
Half an hour later, I got to work; my telephone rang.
"I change me plan." "No bother with the fish."
"I'll buy, and fry them fish myself."
"That way I will get much more
so I can give Gloria some."

And so at twilight that afternoon
the fish was bought, ready to be fried,
well-seasoned and soaked.
Black pepper, Adobo, all-purpose seasoning—
a little of this, a little of that, and a pinch of Mrs. Dash.
Just like the old West Indian days,
we make good with what we've got.

"Come with me, round a Gloria yard."
"Make we go fry them fish."
"Her backyard is more private,
nobody to look inside me Dutch pot."
"Woman! Me tired. Me have to get some sleep.
I will join you later on, in the night,
to help you turn that frying pot."

Late that night, I drove my van
to meet my West Indian wife
round a Canarsie in Gloria backyard,
caught her in the act—under the big green shed
frying the living daylight out of them little fish.
Fire blazing hot like hell, sizzling to an island crisp.
Croaker, porgy, snapper, small whitening,
green parrot and herring sprat.

W. Henry Eccleston

West Indian satisfaction to the max.

Whey Gloria de, "She's had her fill, then left for work."
"Garnet is keeping me—company."
"He's gone inside the house
to remove a fry fish bone, fasten in his throat."
"Excuse me," I cried, jumped back in my van,
drove to the Korean–West Indian vegetable stand,
bought two Trinidadian bread, then headed back to the home.
There, Garnet sat catching warmth from the heated coal-
fire blaze, hot as hell, Garnet peeping in the pot,
keeping Tina's company—the frying fish under watch.

Garnet ate two slices of bread
loosening the bone from his throat.
Itine push—the poker under the hot Dutch pot,
poking up the fire to keep the heat proper.
The pot of coconut oil, heated to a sizzle.
Onions—red, green, and golden sweet peppers,
sliced, sautéing and simmering in the pot.
A little vinegar sprinkled over it adds flavor to the fish,
done just right—fit for any Caribbean king.

REMNANT OF THE ERA DAYS

Hardly any logwood fire sticks left to blaze.
The red hot coal and ashes remain bare.
Our council hardly gathers with sacrament of smoke
though still fierce the cause appears to be
while hustling daily, carving out a livelihood.

With the ideology just a shadow of yesterday's,
when the council was stronger and more fearsome:
long mane, woolly natty bongo dreadlocks they still wear
as the old lions slowly disappear,
more shedding their mane.

The "younglings" are needed to be forceful as in former times,
when Rudies carried a cultured fight for the cause.
All that's left now, it appears, are remnants—of ganja sacrament,
symbols of cultured yards,
landmarks—and outstretched palms coaxing harms,
reminiscing with tourists—the heroes of our once era days.

W. Henry Eccleston

IMAGES OF THE HEART

Within the walls of Bar Reis's room
every one listens to what Heather says!
In dim light, she reads this, revealing that
the messages your palm lines have got
form the flow of lines etched in your hands.
She'll tell you the cosmic path you're sailing on.

The graceful play of her soul this night
leaped from her body taking its flight.
On cold stone ground her soul did lay,
pulling the body there—to laughter, fun and play.
What awesome moments she displayed,
break dancing on the concrete floor
among the tables, chairs, and doors.

Within her gleeful throbbing heart
beating beneath her stunning breasts,
I remembered her for much cheerfulness!
From impressionable-imaged moments
radiating from her figure, a glowing face,
which her precious soul did so impart.

VIRTUE

Forces are there
holding my life in check,
pulling my being in directions
foreign and unknown.
Like repelling strength of magnets
they claim the sway,
the emptiness. A widened void
remains bare for display.
Had I need of opportunities that bring opposed virtues,
which suit my ego at best?
Giving rise to high and noble cause,
I seek for that which opposes.
It seems very weak.
What passion drives vulnerability in check?
The tattered thread stitches across my weakened mind.
Yet in opposites I find strength.
Resourceful substance gaining the effect.

W. Henry Eccleston

REGGAE ROCKS

Just so well the groove is right
bubbling on the acoustic flight
pushing thumb against the strings
vibrating numbness deep within.
Family holding the gaming plays
while bodies move during their stay.

The music first will numb your mind
stinging, shivering down your spine.
Within your bones the base line crawls
tantalizing your rhythmic soul.
Reggae rocks you to and fro
a mellow mood this blessed night.

Plucking strings like rag doll dancing
puppetry strung and pushing the bodies their
agitating the wild—commanding, do your thing!
Carle slaps the cowhide skin
setting the rhythmic pattern flowing
beating the pedal beneath his topping foot.

IMMORTAL'S WILL

The immortal's will, manifest itself
spoken for the day.
We, who've been lost, shall have found our way,
conditioning thoughts frozen to display.
Whatever mode that shapes our every day
through the vial of darkness we may find our place.
If the light and sound we seek so brightly shine
illuminates the way, to a brighter day.
We shall accomplish the task at hand, plain for all to see,
whatever tasks destiny has demand.

W. Henry Eccleston

RASTA CO SHARES A CHURCH

One aim,
    One love,
        One heart,
            One destiny
throbbing under ethereal clouds, the mood,
the flow of cosmic consciousness pulsating
flowing through human cultural senses, beneath
church cathedral skies.
Chanting voices, echoes of love filled the air.
His words of emancipation vying everywhere.
He is ours, he help us free our minds.
His music, so soothing, yet like raspy sand paper
rubbing; erasing the dross embedded deep inside.
His natural mystic vibrations touching wary souls
strung across the four corners of this Universe.
First cry in Nine Miles, message formed in Trench Town
vibrating throughout the reggae land
catapult everywhere, with mortals embracing his word.
The burning desires of a community board
touched the tip of a Barron's pen
with substance of glee in the eagle's eye.
New York. New York. Brooklyn has complied
warming the heart of graceful mayoral thoughts.
Jubilation flares when the preacher said, "Let's hold hands.
I shall ask God to seal this cultural sacrament
an Avenue shared, co-hosting the Rasta man
with drums drumming, steel pans panning
The message music of the mystic one."
Jubilant youth, with spurts of dancing in the street
tiny tots, chanting voices harmonizing words of his wisdom
parental guidance displayed, approval of one love
flashing dread locks shows strength across cultural lines.

Dignitaries, from every land raised their voices giving blessings
echoed cries of sentiments with strength of love overflowing.
A church cathedral avenue co-shared its edifice
a Rasta man, his Boulevard, co-exist.
                                            "Bob Marley" Rasta Lives!

W. Henry Eccleston

THE PLAYGROUND OF SOULS

The privilege is there.
To my soul's desire
knowing then, at will I can float away
and share in joy, the play of souls today
to join the clan, the sparks of God
emanating from the creator's loving hands.

Retracted from this solid form
the mansion here on earth below
there were mind, brain, and affected senses
beyond space,
time and earth matter world.
It has devised my privilege
but for a while,
I bask and frolic in happiness there.
That land, where my soul knows so well
the stream, rivers, oceans of tranquility—
In that place, the home
souls shall come again to dwell
the privilege we'll earn from the journeys of cause-effects.

YOUR SWEET ORCHID

Come, let me cover your sweet orchid
with Egyptian linen so fine,
cradling you beneath its gentle, yet tender shade sublime.
Let me wrap that tender orchid
with fine Kashmir silky, silk, covering, still, just the same.

You let me cover your sculptured breast with fine black beaded triacetate
your lower torso fitted with black rayon, rare, and so fine.
You let me cover your delicate feet with black strap suede from Sicily.
You let me spray your sweet body with scented lavender, flavored by Victoria's Secret Possibilities.
And covering your toes which were so natural, now painted in flaming, gaming, fire red.
Oh! How beautiful you appear this night,
with combination so rare in that soft, sweet, yet so delicate light.

So why then, did you not trust me, to cover you delicate, sweet orchid
with pure silk and fine linen, so rear?
I swear! I will neither touch its tender petals nor taste of its dainty buds.
This will be my solemn promise. I swear!
My dear, unless you deemed it, otherwise.

W. Henry Eccleston

GOD'S LEISURE TIME

You are a smart one! God,
hide yourself in a clay temple
and choose—call it man.
I can hardly say its divide and conquer
for it is more than just that.
When I take a stack—observing deep within
looking for the reasons you did that
somehow, I think you're a weary lonely being
needing to have someone to talk to, and share with.
Like, when them Wall Street executives
work in their big job, way up in them skyscrapers
and then get bored
needing to lighten up somehow and
shoot the breeze a while.
So they go, hang out somewhere else
with some friends
where the stress is less, then kill a little time.
The good thing about it though is
selflessness caused you to give man
free will, and place in him the imprint
of your ways, stamping it on his inward parts
so all that is within you, is in man.
And all that is in him is within you.
Whatever you share with man, most things
you still did not give him access to know.
For man, up to now, has not conquered your ways
nor even fathomed your every thought
Whatever there is, you build it; with
whichever techniques you use.
Some say it is through evolution
Others speculate; you use other means.
I am not debating that right now.

It isn't my purpose and place
nor my true concern.
Some say you love soul, so you allowed it
giving it longevity, pickled its levity
to see what would come of it, or what
would become of its outgrowth.
Look what we souls have done
with those gifts you endowed.
Is this a blessing you curse us with?
Or a curse that you bless us with?
 Look what we have done with it!
And then you walk away—intending
to be back again some day,
leaving everything intact.
What soup have we created—Man!
O what have we done to your game?
You've started, so long ago—
with the tools left behind.
They began to abuse each another
In the wrong kind of ways: killing, hoarding.
Deceitfulness crept in, and chaos began.
Life dealt her gifts in increments.
Where have the years gone, so swiftly?
It is as though, it was yesterday
I stood in memory's thoughts, at this point in time
looking for the next move to make
as progress does demand.
Thinking, when will you come again?
When you get bored—again? Again?

W. Henry Eccleston

EMBATTLED FIELDS AT GETTYSBURG

Embattled fields at Gettysburg:
The Civil War raged on.
Mountain regions, shielded protection lying row by row.
Observation towers—Culp's Hill, soldiers hid in swales low
The Union Blue—the Souther Grey, collided near Devil's Den,
fought a bloody battle for the cause, establishing effects
Fish-hook formations plot, robbed men and beasts of their souls.
Spiked-row fences, stone wall barriers kept fighting men at bay.
Open fields—parched brown earth of greenery surrounded
dug-out trenches, opposing forces—men charged toward their foe.
High above mountain ridges, defenders of the cause.
Craggy-Rock Creek, boulders spread strategically on hillside moan.
Nature sets her course defending
the troop's formation held at Spangler's spring.
Strategically held possessions—the battle raged on.
Troops gave chase at Little Round Top, blasted cannon fire.
Low-ground disadvantage gave way to fallen men.
Divisions—everywhere, thousands perished—establishing new
cause.
Thick as blood, good men of faith—against brothers' will—
amended.
The blue haze vaporized—spread across sacred fields
transformed, where ideology build defenses.
Liberated! Consciousness expansion, souls of faith set free.
The Union Flag unfurled—one external flame kept burning,
connected, the Blue with the Confederate Grey.

TRANSFORMED TRENCH PEN- CREATING TRENCH TOWN

British colonial settlers' while fulfilling there dreams –
In her commonwealth of nations, a Scottish planter seeks
 Opportunity knocks he staked his conquered claim
Acquired properties accomplishing his desires - hoped to
Someday make a better life on this chosen foreign soil -
Future fortune under disguise of advancing his race
 Emancipation induces abolition marked ways for a
Brighter day, at the cross roads poverty meets plenty.
Cashia macca wildly growing as though it's a crown of
Thorns, strapped around our dull browed mind; like
The Genesis story of thistles and sweat to eat our bread.
Tumble weeds turning brown, shrubs and
Burr bush flourishes in cluster scattered patches
Tumble bugs rolling whatever is enticingly
Found lying in plenty, on cold damp ground
Ground lizards crawl leaving trail of markings
From there bellies, feet and tails pressed down
 By slow movements' etched in loose soil.
Rodents crawls feeding on insects, searching for
A morsel or a crumb to feed there burrowed kin
Ground doves and small birds peck at open padded
 Seeds and small things that can be found
Domesticated hogs drift, while heard of goats
 And cattle Roamed about scavenging,
  Eating garbage and paper, piling on waste heap.
Shanties like shacks, thickens in cluster as
Squatters' stake choice claims on parceled lands
 And government low income houses in tenement yards.
Largest in ambition beaten down repelling poverty
In peoples lives, while hoping for a brighter future.
Life forms culture in our town, surviving on our own

W. Henry Eccleston

So must we in conclusion music is, our true art form-
Dubbed us becoming capital of the Reggae world
Musicologists', writers and foreign journalists penned
How exceptionality becomes us from Trench Town.
Disgruntle opulence in lack, rebellious short comings
Internalize hoping for benefits privilege have,
Have haves, and have not displayed. ~Ganja splif and
Loaded chillum pipes, savors as religious sacrament
Symbolizing repatriation of back to Africa with
Marcus Mosiah Garvey looking to the East from
Where our redemption shall come. Africa –
Oh! Mama Africa –* "Ethiopia shall soon stretch
Out her hands unto God". A crown King had given hope
To our prophets through remnants, in Redemption songs.

* Psalm: 68 – v: 31